A POCKET GUIDE TO
kids are worth it!

GIVING YOUR CHILD THE GIFT
OF INNER DISCIPLINE

BARBARA
COLOROSO

SOMERVILLE HOUSE PUBLISHING
TORONTO

ISBN: 1-894042-08-5

Cover Design: Andrew Smith Graphics

Cover Photography: Monty Nuss

Printed in China

Published by Somerville House Publishing,
a division of Somerville House Books Limited,
3080 Yonge Street, Suite 5000,
Toronto, Ontario M4N 3N1

Somerville House Publishing acknowledges the financial assistance of the Ontario Publishing Centre, the Ontario Arts Council, the Ontario Development Corporation, and the Department of Communications.

To Anna, Maria, and Joseph
I wish for each one of you
the gentle joy that comes
with justice seeking
and peacemaking

Contents

One
kids are worth it! 7

Two
Three Kinds of Families 27

Three
*Three Alternatives to No and
Other Plan Bs* 37

Four
I Can Be Me. 41

Five
*Keeping Your Cool Without
Putting Your Feelings on Ice* . . 47

Six
*Realities, Mistakes,
and Problems* 61

Seven
*Getting Your Kid Out of Jail
and Other Mega-Problems* . . . 71

Eight
Settling Sibling Rivalry 75

Nine
The Big C and the Three Rs:
Chores, Relaxation, Recreation,
and Rebellion. 83

Ten
Money Matters. 97

Eleven
Mealtime 109

Twelve
Bedtime Doesn't Have to Be a
Nightmare 117

Thirteen
Ready, Sit, Go —
Toilet Training 123

Fourteen
Sexuality is Not a
Four-Letter Word. 131

Epilogue. 143

One
kids are worth it!

... because they are children and for no other reason, they have dignity and worth simply because they are. They don't need to prove their value as human beings; they don't have to prove their worthiness to us; nor do they need to earn our affection.

Believing kids are worth it, not treating them in a way I would not want to be treated, and behaving in a way that leaves our dignity intact are not themselves specific tools; rather, they provide an attitude and an environment that helps me help my children develop a sense of self-discipline.

Philosophical Tenets

1. Kids are worth it.
2. I will not treat a child in a way I myself would not want to be treated.
3. If it works and leaves a child's and my own dignity intact, do it.

The Golden Rule, as it is called, can serve us well when applied to our relations with our children. If we are not sure whether what we are doing with children is right, we need only put ourselves in their place and ask if we would want it done to us–not *was* it done to us, but *would we want it done to us?* If the answer is no, then we have to ask ourselves why we would ever want to do it to our children.

I believe that for the first time in our history we have the tools necessary to break cycles of dysfunction, abuse, and neglect. We now have the individual and collective awareness of the damages that physical and emotional abuse can cause a child, a family, and a society.

Once we are committed to the idea that we will not treat our children in a way we ourselves would not want to be treated, we can begin to find responsible, effective alternatives to the punitive tools of threatening, hitting, psychologically or verbally abusing, neglecting, or abandoning our children.

Kids who are consistently bribed and rewarded are likely to grow into adults who are overly dependent on others for approval and recognition, lacking their own self-confidence and sense of responsibility.

The questions they will often ask are:

- What's in it for me?
- What's the payoff?
- Does it count for anything?
- Do you like it?
- Did you see me do it?
- Did I do it right?

Threats and punishments are by their nature punitive; they are adult-oriented, are based on judgment, and impose power from without instead of acknowledging the power within children. They arouse anger and resentment and invite more conflict. Most important, they rob a child of his sense of dignity and self-worth.

Threats and punishments can take the form of:

Isolation

Embarrassment and humiliation

Shaming

Emotional isolation

Grounding

Brute force

16

Faced with domination, manipulation, and control by someone bigger than themselves, children will experience one of three things:

1. Fright—doing as they are told out of dependency and fear.

2. Fight—attacking the adult or taking the anger out on others.

3. Flight—running away mentally or physically.

...to discipline with authority means to give life to learning. Our goal as parents is to give life to our children's learning—to teach, to instruct, to help them develop self-discipline—an ordering of the self from the inside, not imposition from the outside.

18

4 Steps of Discipline

1. Shows kids what they have done.
2. Gives them ownership of the problem.
3. Gives them options for solving the problem.
4. Leaves their dignity intact.

Encouragement inspires. It imparts courage and confidence. It fosters and gives support. It helps a child develop a sense of self-pride and enhances internal motivation. Encouraging a child means that one or more of the following critical life messages are coming through either by word or by action:

- I believe in you.
- I trust you.
- I know you can handle this.
- You are listened to.
- You are cared for.
- You are very important to me.

Empowering our children involves first giving them a secure, safe, nurturing environment–offering them unconditional love, caring touch, tenderness, and concern for their physical, emotional and spiritual well-being.

22

With a strong loving foundation in place we can begin to give our children the opportunity to make choices and decisions, all the while providing a structure on which they can build, increasing their responsibilities and decision-making opportunities as they grow.

Just as RSVP is a request for a response, a consequence that is reasonable, simple, valuable, and practical will invite a responsible action from your child. When in doubt about a consequence, you can check if all four clues are present:

1. **R** — Is it reasonable?
2. **S** — Is it simple?
3. **V** — Is it valuable as a learning tool?
4. **P** — Is it practical?

If it isn't all four of these, it probably won't be effective and it could be punishment disguised as a reasonable consequence.

Real-world consequences either happen naturally or are *reasonable* consequences that are intrinsically related to the child's actions. Real-world consequences teach children about the world around them and that they themselves have positive control of their lives. They can make decisions and solve problems.

26

Two
Three Kinds of Families

There are three basic kinds of families: brick-wall, jellyfish, and backbone. What distinguishes them is the kind of structure that holds them together....A brick-wall is a non-living thing, designed to restrict, to keep in, and to keep out....A jellyfish has no firm parts at all and reacts to every eddy and current that comes along....A backbone is a living supple spine that gives form and movement to the whole body.

28

Brick-wall Family Checklist

1. Hierarchy of control.

2. Litany of strict rules.

3. Punctuality, cleanliness, and order.

4. Rigid enforcement of rules by means of actual threatened, or imagined, violence.

5. Attempt to break the child's will and spirit with fear and punishment.

6. Rigid rituals and rote learning.

7. Use of humiliation.

8. Extensive use of threats and bribes.

9. Heavy reliance on competition.

10. Learning takes place in an atmosphere of fear.

11. Love is highly conditional.

12. Separate, strictly enforced roles.

13. Teach what to think, not how to think.

14. Risk of sexual promiscuity, drug abuse, and suicide.

15. Refuses to acknowledge the need to get help.

Jellyfish Family Checklist

1. Anarchy and chaos in the physical and emotional environment.

2. No recognizable structure, rules, or guidelines.

3. Arbitrary and instant punishments and rewards.

4. Mini lectures and put-downs and tools of the trade.

5. Second chances are arbitrarily given.

6. Threats and bribes are commonplace.

7. Everything takes place in an environment of chaos.

8. Emotions rule the behavior of parents and children.

9. Children are taught that love is highly conditional.

10. Children are easily led by their peers.

11. Risk of sexual promiscuity, drug abuse, and suicide.

12. Parents are oblivious to major family problems, and fail to recognize the need to seek help.

Backbone Family Checklist

1. Parents develop for their children a network of support through six critical life messages given every day.

2. Democracy is learned through experience.

3. An environment is created that is conducive to creative, constructive, and responsible activity.

4. Rules are simply and clearly stated.

5. Consequences for irresponsible behavior are either natural or reasonable.

6. Discipline is handled with authority that gives life to children's learning.
7. Children are motivated to be all they can be.
8. Children receive lots of smiles, hugs, and humor.
9. Children get second opportunities.
10. Children learn to accept their own feelings and to act responsibly on those feelings through a strong sense of self-awareness.
11. Competency and cooperation are modeled and encouraged.

12. Love is unconditional.
13. Children are taught how to think.
14. Children are buffered from sexual promiscuity, drug abuse, and suicide by the daily reinforcement of the messages that foster self-esteem:

> I like myself.
> I can think for myself.
> There is no problem so great, it can't be solved.

15. The family is willing to seek help.

The backbone family provides the support and structure necessary for children to realize fully their uniqueness and to come to know their true selves, which are suppressed in brick-wall families and ignored in jellyfish families. They are empowered by trust in themselves, in others, and in the future. Being secure in their own unique selves, they are capable of love and empathy for themselves and others. Backbone families help children develop inner discipline, and even in the face of adversity and peer pressure, they retain faith in themselves and in their own potential.

Three

Three Alternatives to No
And Other Plan B's

Save your no for the big issues, when you really mean No! The rest of the time, as the no begins to form on your lips, stop a moment and see if one of the alternatives might better serve both you and your kids:

1. "Yes, later."
2. "Give me a minute."
3. "Convince me."

Backbone parents save their no for the big issues, when there is no bend, when they mean it, intend to follow through with it, and it is in the best interest of the safety and well-being of the child. With the no they give an explanation that is meaningful. Children can then begin to develop their own internal moral structure that enables them to function responsibly and creatively in society.

Self-trust is one of the first steps toward becoming a responsible, resourceful, resilient human being. Children don't need many nos, any mini lectures, unnecessary questions, empty threats, ultimatums, put-downs, warnings, or dictates.
What they do need is support, explanations, encouragement, opportunities to be responsible, and invitations to think for themselves.

Four

I Can Be Me

If you want your kids to make wise choices, give them the opportunity to make lots of choices—including some unwise ones.

If a situation is neither life-threatening, morally threatening, nor unhealthy ask yourself if the natural consequence of what your child is doing would give life to your child's learning.

If the answer is yes, stay out of it and let nature take its course.

Teaching them to make their own decisions enables them to learn to be responsible individuals who can act in their own best interest, stand up for themselves, and exercise their own rights while respecting the rights and legitimate needs of others.

44

There are some decisions and responsibilities that parents need to keep for themselves. Different parents will make different choices. But first a parent needs to ask: Am I keeping this decision or responsibility for myself because I am afraid to give it to my kids for fear of losing control, or because it is a part of being a wise and caring parent?

An excellent way to teach the art of decision making is to let kids make decisions, guide them through the process without passing judgment, and let them grow through the results of their decisions. Mistakes and poor choices then become a child's own responsibility. The hurt or discomfort arising from the choices will only go away after the child has worked out the problem constructively. By having power over the situation, the child's dignity, integrity, and self-worth are enhanced.

46

Five
Keeping Your Cool Without
Putting Your Feelings On Ice

Kids need to know it's all right to feel. It is all right to be happy, concerned, joyful, sad, angry, frustrated, and hurt. Feelings are motivators for growth or warning signs that something needs changing. When we are concerned or joyful, we have energy to grow and to extend ourselves outward. When we are angry or hurt, our feelings are signaling our mind and body that something is not right and needs to be changed. Sometimes what needs changing is not the situation itself but our view of it.

In jellyfish families kids are not taught how to identify or responsibly express their feelings. Often the adults express their own feelings and respond to their child's feelings in extreme ways. The parent will either smother the child and try to own the feelings for her, not encouraging her to work through her own feelings. Or the parent will totally disregard the child's feelings through abandonment or neglect.

In brick-wall families, kids are taught not to express their true feelings, their true selves. Forbidden to express emotions themselves, kids get stuck in their anger, fear, sadness, and hurt. The energy builds up inside, like steam pressure in a boiler.

Eventually one of three things results:

1. Passive-destructive acts against the self

2. Aggressive acts against others

3. Passive-aggressive acts (a combination of the other two)

Parents in a backbone family regularly do five things:

1. They acknowledge their own feelings and label them.

2. They admit that they are angry, or hurt, or afraid, then do something responsible and purposeful to address these feelings.

3. They make assertive statements about themselves.

4. They acknowledge their children's feelings as real and legitimate, without passing judgment on those feelings.

5. They teach their children to handle their own feelings assertively.

If a child learns that his feelings are accepted as real and legitimate and he is helped to express them in words and to act on them responsibly when he is in the first age of rebellion, he will find it easier to adapt those skills to the challenges of the next two stages of rebellion.

54

Tough as it is, it is easier to be
patient with a two-year-old
who is throwing a temper
tantrum than with a teenager
doing the same thing. Yet he
needs the same help labeling
his feelings and figuring out
a constructive way to
handle them.

It takes time to teach kids to handle their feelings assertively, but in doing so you teach them that their own feelings are important, that they can be trusted to handle those feelings, and that they can count on you for support and guidance when they have handled them poorly.

Seven Steps for a Fair Fight

1. When you are upset or angry, say so in an upset or angry tone of voice.

2. Tell the other person about your feelings.

3. State your belief out loud but avoid killer statements.

4. Close the time gap between the hurt and the expression of that hurt. Give direct feedback.

5. State what you want from the other person.

6. Be open to the other person's perspective on the situation.

7. Negotiate an agreement you can both accept.

Both children and adults need to recognize that to *keep* it a fair fight, it is always acceptable to

1. Call time out.
2. Refuse to take abuse.
3. Insist on fair treatment.

Fighting fair enables parents and kids to use their feelings as a positive energy source to establish and maintain productive relationships with one another and with other people outside the family.

60

Six
Realities, Mistakes
and Problems

A backbone parent admits that she made a mistake, takes full responsibility for making the mistake, avoids making excuses, figures out how to fix the problem created by making the mistake, recognizes if, and how, another person was affected, and figures out what to do the next time so it won't happen again.

You often can't control what happens to you, but what you can do is use what is happening to you. A big part of using what is happening to you is distinguishing between what can be changed and what has to be accepted.

We can empower kids by giving them the message "You have a problem; I know you can solve it." We can destroy their sense of dignity and self-worth by giving them the message "You have a problem, but I don't think you can solve it." Or an even worse message: "You don't have a problem: you *are* the problem."

It's easy to give these negative messages without even realizing it especially if we were raised with those messages from our own parents. It takes conscious effort and constant awareness to give the positive message.

Six Steps to Problem Solving

1. Identify and define the problem.
2. List viable options for solving the problem.
3. Evaluate the options— explore the pluses and minuses for each option.
4. Choose one option.
5. Make a plan and DO IT.
6. Evaluate the problem and your solution: What brought it about? Could a similar problem be prevented in the future? How was the present problem solved?

A family meeting can be a forum for kids to learn to examine situations, propose solutions, and evaluate the results with guidance, support, and demonstrations from parents and older siblings. It is an opportunity to reinforce the notion that the goal for our children is not dependence or independence but rather a sense of interdependence. We are all connected; what we do or not do influences and affects those around us.

Three basic requirements for
a family meeting

1. The problem must be
   important and relevant to
   all concerned.

2. The parent needs to provide
   nonjudgmental leadership.

3. The environment needs to be
   conducive to sharing.

Having presented their own ideas, listened to one another's reasoning, and worked cooperatively to arrive at a solution, all family members begin to see that there is no definite right or wrong, no one correct way to solve most problems. Group choices involve give-and-take, openness, and cooperation on the part of all concerned.

If we parents accept that problems are an essential part of life's challenges, rather than reacting to every problem as if something has gone wrong with a universe that's supposed to be perfect, we can demonstrate serenity and confidence in problem solving for our kids. We can teach them that no problem is so great that it can't be solved.

Seven

Getting Your Kid Out of Jail
and Other Mega-Problems

As their whole world is crashing in on them, what kids do need is someone to stand behind them and tell them, "I believe in you. I trust you. I know you can handle this. You are listened to, cared for, and very important to me. We aren't concerned with what the rest of the community is saying. We love you and we're here—not to rescue, blame, or punish but to support and discipline."

All of our kids will make mistakes; that's part of growing up. Growing up can be painful, and it's hard for us to see our children in pain. But let the mistakes and poor choices become your kids' own responsibility. That doesn't mean you stand back and let them destroy their lives ... Just as you might restrain an angry toddler who was hell-bent on hurting himself or his younger brother, you might have to get professional help to restrain a drug-crazed son or to

intravenously feed an anorexic daughter. The intervention and control is only temporary and will need to give way to the teens' eventually taking ownership of their own problems and the solutions to those problems ...

By having positive power over even such painful situations as mega-problems, their dignity, integrity, and self-worth are enhanced.

74

Eight
Sibling Rivalry Without Calling in the Cavalry

Kids fight. The next time your kids are going at it, take a big breath and tell yourself, "They're normal." Conflict is inevitable, as much a part of life as sleeping, eating and paying taxes. So is the pain that goes along with it. But you can resolve conflict and make it less painful if you deal with it directly and creatively.

Example is a powerful way of teaching our kids to handle conflict. Kids tend to handle it the way they see us handle it. If we were lucky enough to see significant people in our lives handle conflict assertively, without aggression or passivity, we can model for our children the same behavior.

When given the proper tools, kids can and do come up with a productive plan to solve their own conflict. With young children you may have to give them options they can choose from. As they grow older, one of three things will likely happen:

1. They will share.

2. They will both get up and leave, finding something else to do.

3. One of them will come up with a plan they both agree to.

Instead of bombarding children with the message that aggression is the way to resolve conflict, we as adults can teach, through example, guidance, and instruction, that violence is an immature, irresponsible, and unproductive technique to resolve conflict and that using nonviolent tools to resolve conflict is a mature and courageous act.

I believe that if we are to survive as a planet, we must teach this next generation to handle their own conflicts assertively and nonviolently. If in their early years our children learn to listen to all sides of the story, use their heads and then their mouths, and come up with a plan and share, then, when they become our leaders, and some of them will, they will have the tools to handle global problems and conflicts.

It's going to take example, guidance, and instruction from us to impart to our children the wisdom of peacemakers:

Violence is "the knot of bondage"; aggression only begets more aggression; passivity invites it; and assertion can dissipate it. Peace is not the absence of conflict. It is the embracing of conflict as a challenge and an opportunity to grow.

Knowing how to handle conflict is more than a matter of creating peace in the home; it is a matter of creating a peaceful attitude in ourselves and our children so that we can create that peaceful atmosphere in our home.

82

Nine

The Big C and the Three Rs:
Chores, Relaxation,
Recreation and Rebellion

Chores and leisure activity are the yin and yang of a strong personal and family backbone. The two cannot be viewed separately from each other, since the interplay between them created a whole … A strong backbone that is at once stable and flexible cannot be developed by emphasizing one or the other.

Kids are more likely to do chores willingly if they feel that we truly need and welcome their help, that we are not simply giving them chores to teach them lessons or because we don't want to do the work ourselves. That means we have to present ordinary chores in such a way that they are meaningful to a child, useful for the family, and part of the harmonious order of our home.

Children need to believe that they can make a contribution, can make a difference in their families.

86

Ordinary chores...can help kids:

- Develop the ability to organize their own resources.
- Experience closure on tasks.
- Organize themselves.
- Set goals and build skills necessary to work through more complex physical and mental tasks.

If you want your children to learn a skill, do it yourself. Demonstrate for them first, then teach them. Guide them through it, and then let them do it on their own.

There are lots of ways to do chores. It doesn't always have to be my way. Be willing to give a bit. This is *our* home. We can do it in *our* way and in *our* time. Figuring out how to do this will mean communicating with one another, making our expectations clear, and listening carefully to one another.

For children to grow in the sense of inner discipline, they need time to be alone and still .... As a backbone parent, taking the time every day to be still yourself will give you the opportunity to "be guided a little more by your gut." By encouraging your children to "sit down, be quiet, and get to like yourself" you will be giving them the opportunity to tap into their own intuition.

Play is more than the absence of work or the reward for work well done. It is not something that has to be earned. It is an opportunity to re-create and renew ourselves, and connect with others in the spirit of cooperation and acceptance.

If our goal is to raise children up to survive in the real world and make it a better place, it would serve us well to examine our cultural attitudes toward play, games, and organized sports. We can choose to raise our children to be competent, cooperative, and decisive individuals, who, if they want to, or have to compete, will do so with a moral sense.

92

Get out with your kids for no
other reason than to delight in
one another's company.
You will find that play can
renew and refresh and
reconnect each one of you.

It is not enough to practice the art of meditation—to be alone and quiet, reflective and silent, cooperative and seeking harmony in relationships. To be wholly human is to balance this inner journey with the art of resistance. Our children need to be able to see us take a stand *for* a value and *against* injustices, be those values and injustices in the family room, the boardroom, the classroom, or on the city streets.

When we do more than give lip service to our "passionate priorities," when we walk our talk, we model for our children ways to rebel and resist creatively, constructively, and responsibly.

The greatest part of each day, each year, each lifetime is made up of small, seemingly insignificant moments. Every time a child organizes and completes a chore, spends some time alone without feeling lonely, loses herself in play for an hour, or refuses to go along with her peers in some activity she feels is wrong, she will be building meaning and a sense of worth for herself and harmony in her family.

96

Ten
Money Matters

Since my children are not paid for everyday chores, I am often asked if I ever give my children money. Yes, I do give them an allowance for three reasons: to learn how to handle money, to make decisions about their own money, and to set financial priorities.

What is important for kids to learn is that no matter how much money they have, earn, win, or inherit, they need to know how to spend it, how to save it, and how to give to others in need.

In deciding how much allowance to give our kids, we need to ask ourselves four questions:

1. How much can I afford?
2. How much do I want to give?
3. How much can my child handle? It needs to be enough not to frustrate the child but not so much that no responsible choices need to be made or priorities set.
4. What does my child need the money for?

Given the choice, children who don't want for anything will not save. And many children today don't want for anything.

We have an obligation as parents to give our children *what they need*. What they want we can give them as a special gift, or they can save their money for it.

When charitable giving in the form of money becomes a habit, kids can then become aware of giving of their time and their talents as well.

When children start earning money for "out of the ordinary jobs" at home or for work in the neighborhood, they can start contributing to their long-term as well as short-term savings.

103

After giving and saving, the rest of the money may be spent on things that are not life-threatening, morally threatening, or unhealthy. You can allow a lot of freedom to a young kid to buy what is meaningful to her. She will begin to develop her own backbone in understanding and using money.

104

When a child begins to
recognize the difference
between needs and wants,
bare necessities, amenities,
and luxuries the structure
for responsible money habits
is being developed.

The backbone parent does not lend money frivolously and for every occasion but recognizes that there are times when any of us may need to take out a loan and repay it later.

You have a special problem if you have a wealthy or generous relative or parent who sends large sums of money to you children ... This can undermine all the effort you put into teaching your kids to handle money. You as a backbone parent should send a note to the relative or parent along with deposit slips for your child's long-term savings account and suggest, for the child's sake, that they send a small amount of money to the children and put the rest in the long-term account.

When do you increase the allowance? Simple—when your kids can convince you that they *need* a bigger allowance.

Eleven

Mealtime

There is something profoundly satisfying about sharing a meal. Eating together, breaking bread together, is one of the oldest and most fundamentally unifying of human experiences.

As food nourishes the body, food eaten in company also nourishes the individual spirit, the family, the community, and the world. The harmony of a meal eaten together spreads far beyond the table and far beyond mealtime.

If you can get your young children to talk with you at meals, they will still talk to you when they reach the teen years, since they will have learned that mealtime is a safe time for sharing.

Backbone parents provide a healthy and flexible structure for mealtime. It is a celebration, an occasion to come together as a family to nourish the body, mind, and soul. It is also a time to teach children about nutrition, food preparation, manners, and conversation or dialogue—the mutual exchange of ideas, opinions, and feelings.

Food conflicts can be reduced by following a few simple guidelines:

- Have a variety of good foods in the house and eat those foods yourself.

- Teach your children about the food they are eating.

- Let your children help plan and prepare well-balanced meals and nutritious snacks.

- Eat a variety of meals served a variety of ways.

- At least once a month have a formal celebration with your children.

- Teach your children cultural or religious customs that have been in your families for years.

- Teach your kids manners, not etiquette.

- Teach your children how to shop for groceries.

- Teach your children to cook.

We need to take time in our busy lives today to celebrate mealtime with our children. It would be wonderful if an adult in a kid's life shared at least one meal a day with her ....
Even more exciting would be if the whole family could find a special time each day to come together and share food, good thoughts, and lively discussion.

Twelve

Bedtime Doesn't Have to Be a Nightmare

Basically what has to be established is a bed time, bed place, and bedtime routine.

As a family you have to look together at what works best in your home. You have to do what you can live with, set what works for your family, and be open and flexible to the changing sleep needs and routines of the members of your family.

Backbone parents provide a basic bedtime routine that is flexible enough to adjust to the needs of the individual family members and the family as a whole. Responsibility for establishing the routine rests first with the parents, but then, as the children grow older, responsibilities and decisions about bedtime and bedtime routine are increasingly turned over to them. By the time they

leave home, the children have a healthy regard for the need to sleep, an understanding of their own body clock, and respect for the needs of those around them. In the give-and-take of family life they have learned common courtesies and are able to balance their own needs and wants with the needs and wants of those they are living with.

Bedtime is a special time, a time of transition. It is an opportunity for closure to one day and a preparation for the next. It is a small turning point in the natural rhythm that gives structure and meaning to life. Just as the seasons and their holidays and celebrations mark the great natural movements of the years, so bedtime marks the turning of the days. With care and patience and awareness of our children's needs, each bedtime can be its own celebration of love and life.

Thirteen
Ready, Sit, Go-Toilet Training

A brick-wall parent takes ownership of the process of toilet training. She often wants to start the process before the child is physically ready. The child has learned to please in all other areas of life and will try to gain approval from her parent by being successful on the toilet, but after several accidents will become either frustrated or resistant, feeling like a failure or refusing to sit on the toilet at all.

The jellyfish parent has a laissez-faire attitude about the whole process. She provides little if any instruction on how the body functions. That a child might be ready to learn at two is missed by the parent because she doesn't see the signs, doesn't have the energy or patience to structure the task for the child, or is simply not there to provide the consistency, structure, support, the guidance ... Inconsistency only prolongs the toilet-training process.

The backbone parent lets the child be in full control of her body functions and master her own toilet training at her own speed. The parent has a flexible routine, is positive and non-chalant about the routine, expects mistakes and sees them as opportunities to learn, has a relaxed attitude, and is available to help. She is not overly concerned about other adults' expectations and comments.

Both you and your child need to be ready to take on the task of toilet training. You need to be willing and able to give your child time, patience, and encouragement she will need from you. And you need to know why you are helping her. Is it because you are tired of changing diapers, or the preschool won't take her unless she is toilet trained, or your neighbors' son sported training pants months ago? If these are the reasons, take a moment to think again. These might influence you, but the real question is, are you ready to help your child because she is ready to be helped?

The Three Ps are the backbone structure that is used:

1. Prepare

The three clues to readiness are:

- physical development
- willingness to toilet train
- ability to communicate with you

2. Practice

It takes practice for a child to learn to control her bladder and her bowels ... The key to remember is that you are helping her learn to take control of her body.

3. Patience

The power or capacity to endure without complaint something difficult.

Once you and your child embark on the toilet-training adventure, thanks to your willingness to establish a backbone structure of preparedness, practice, and patience, your child will be able to begin to see herself as a competent, resourceful, and responsible person who is learning to treat her own body with dignity and regard.

Fourteen

Sexuality is Not a Four-letter word

Kids learn about their sexuality even if it is not us doing the teaching. But often what they learn is misinformation and misinterpretation, exaggerations, and exploitive notions about their own bodies and bodies of people of the opposite sex.

If we want to be the primary sexuality educators of our children, it is critical that we begin an open communication about sexuality early in our kids' lives so that a positive pattern of communication is established before the hormonal changes of puberty affect our teenagers' thoughts and feelings about their own sexuality.

Backbone parents begin to lay a strong foundation for raising sexually healthy children even before their children are born, by coming to understand their own sexuality and how it is an integral part of their values, morals, emotions, and sexual feelings. Treating your own body, your spouse's body, and your child's body with dignity and respect is the beginning of a lifelong relationship of trust, caring, and nurturing.

134

As your young children begin to locate and explore all of their own body parts, you can begin to establish an open and honest channel of communication by using the proper names for *all* of the body parts.

Teachable moments are simple, ordinary, everyday situations that present opportunities for teaching your young children about sexuality. They present opportunities to impart knowledge, values, and a moral backbone on which your children can build their own sense of themselves as sexual beings.

Girls tend to begin their physical and sexual growth spurt at eleven or twelve, boys at fourteen or fifteen, and emotional development for either can occur before, after, or simultaneously with the physical growth spurt. It's no wonder that the most pressing question is "Am I normal?"

Preteens need to know the detailed facts about sexuality, intimacy, dating, and sexually transmitted diseases. The more knowledge they have now, the better able they will be to make responsible decisions about the expressions of their sexuality later.

138

It is during the "un-age" (ages twelve through fifteen) that the drive to separate from their parents is taken up in earnest. At the same time adolescents are looking for your approval, support, and guidance ... This age is punctuated with raging hormones and simple questions that have complicated answers ... Your teen will probably be wondering about falling in love, crushes, self-pleasuring, homosexuality, intercourse and issues related to wet dreams, periods, and pregnancy.

It is during the ages of sixteen and nineteen that your children will move toward independence in all areas of their lives. Issues that have been touched upon before now command stage front and center:

- Sex—why is something so natural and good so complicated?

- Abstinence—the only sure way to avoid pregnancy and sexually transmitted diseases. Are there other benefits?

- Gynecological exam—what is it and when should I have one?

- AIDS and other sexually transmitted diseases—causes, prevention, signs, and symptoms. Can I trust her if she says I am her first?

- Contraception and safer sex—can the two be mutually exclusive?

- Love and sex—can you be in love without having sexual intercourse?

- Sexual abuse—what is it and how can I avoid it?

- Intimacy and friendship—what's the difference and can I have both?

We are our children's parents until they reach puberty. When they reach puberty, it is time for us to move out of the parenting role to become their mentor, a model and a guide. If we mentor them well in the teen years, in adulthood they can become our friends.

Epilogue

Dear Parents,

After you've been caring, and consistent ... firm and fair ... you've said what you meant and meant what you said and did what you said you were going to do ... you've eliminated sarcasm, ridicule, and embarrassment from your talk with your kids and you've developed a backbone structure around mealtime, bedtime, chores, allowances, fighting— and you are totally exhausted, there is one more thing you can do. After your kids are asleep this evening (it's easier when they are sleeping), walk into their bedrooms, look down at each one of them, and remind yourself that there is one thing you and I as parents cannot do, nor do we want to do if we really think about it, and that's control our children's will—that spirit that lets them be themselves apart from you and me.

They are not ours to possess, control, manipulate, or even to make mind. What they are is what Kahlil Gibran said they were: "Life longing for itself." They are gifts to us. Now, granted some came in very unique packaging, but they are still gifts to us, and we need to treat them as gifts. We need to encourage members of this next generation to become all that they can become, not try to force them to become what we want them to become. Neither we nor they would benefit from this narrow-mindedness. You and I can't even begin to dream the dreams this next generation is going to dream, or answer the questions that will be put to them.

If you want your kids to make wise choices, give them the opportunity to make lots of choices—including some unwise ones. Unless the unwise ones are life-threatening, morally threatening, or

145

unhealthy (in which case you have to intervene), allow them to experience the real-world consequences of their own mistakes and poor choices, as painful as they may be.

When they fall, don't be standing in front of them to rescue, or over them to punish. Be behind them to support and guide them. Give them the six critical life messages: I believe in you... I trust in you... I know you can handle this... you are listened to... you are cared for... and you are very important to me.

If you are going to give your kids these six critical life messages, I have an assignment for each one of you. Model these messages for your children. The best way I know to do this is to take at least a half hour out of your day, every day, and give it to the only person who's going to spend the rest of your life with you—and that's you. You're honestly the only

person you can count on being there when you need you the most. So, take that half hour and do something that says, *I like Me!*

Some of you are probably saying, *Woman, you don't understand—we're talking laundry piled three feet high, dishes stacked in the sink, three kids and one on the way, and you want me to give myself a half hour?* You bet I do, because if you don't, I promise you, nobody else will. You must believe first that you're worth it before you can impress on your kids that they're worth it. So take that half hour and run, pray, read a good book, sit quietly, take a long bath (don't eat a hunk of chocolate cake, or you'll regret it)—do something that says, *I like me.*

When you've done that, you won't find that you're the perfect parent or that you have the best-behaved kids in school or the kids with the highest test scores.

No, if you give yourself that half hour, you're going to find something greater—you're going to find the energy and serenity every day to know three things: *I like myself; I can think for myself; and in parenting today there is no problem so great it can't be solved.* You will find yourself winning at parenting, not beating your kids, not controlling them, not making them mind. Rather, you'll be winning by inviting and encouraging your children to become all that they can become. Which is responsible, resourceful, resilient, loving individuals who have the gift of inner discipline.

You're worth it, and so are they. And if that's not enough reason to take the time to develop a strong backbone in your family today, I'd like to leave you with this last reason: old age. Hopefully, you and I are going to have the opportunity to

grow much older and share our wisdom with the generation in which we are now investing our time, our energy and I believe, in parenting, our very lives.

If we can raise this next generation to believe that they can love themselves and in loving themselves, they can then extend themselves in a loving way to others.

If we can teach them that they can think for themselves, and in thinking for themselves would never allow others—governments or drug dealers or friends—to manipulate them, nor would they choose to manipulate others for their own gain.

If we can teach them that they don't have to be good-looking, bright, thin, and young (that silly medium of exchange in our culture) in order to have dignity and worth, then they will understand that it is

because they are children and for no other reason that they have dignity and worth—simply because they *are*.

If we can teach them to not be so dog-eat-dog competitive, but to be truly competent, cooperative, decisive human beings, who if they need to, want to, have to, or are forced to compete, will do it with a moral sense.

And if we can teach them to solve their own personal, social, and academic, problems, then I believe we will have taught them that, in this world, there is no problem so great that it can't be solved.

If we teach our children these things, then, when you and I are old and this next generation starts making decisions for us and for the next generation they will create, we can trust that the time and energy we spent parenting our children

and developing a strong backbone was well worth it. Thanks to our time and energy and love this next generation will be able to make responsible, caring, loving decisions.

You're worth it! Your kids are worth it!

Joy!

Barbara Coloroso